THE SPIRIT OF HEAVINESS

TIFFANY KAMEI

AND ALL ITS COUSINS

HOW TO OVERCOME:

Depression	Perversion
Lust	Gluttony/ Greed
Anti-Christ	Murder
Poverty	Whoredom

Legals

The information in this book is geared at helping the reader to achieve deliverance and understanding, however, the results are up to the reader. As such, the author is not responsible for any individual's results, since each individual has his or her own measure of faith.

This book is intended to inform, educate and show the reader how to achieve their desired goals of being set free from the Spirit of Heaviness and every other spirit mentioned in this book.

Nevertheless, the buyer releases the author from any form of criminal, civil, or moral litigation due to individual results.

Author exercises First Amendment right.

Warning: Demons will HATE this book. May cause deliverance to take place.

Authored by: Tiffany Buckner- Kameni
Edited by: B. Davinia Gordon

ISBN-10:
0-615-56977-3
ISBN-13:
978-0-615-56977-2

Note From the Author

Dear Believer,

Thank you so much for purchasing and reading this publication. I truly bless GOD for your life, but more than anything; I am just blessed and humbled by HIS decision to use me to bring forth this Rhema Word.

I woke up on February 27, 2012, thinking it was going to be a day like every other day, but after an intensely scary nightmare, the LORD took me directly into writing. I then thought that HE would have me to write an article; just a few pages and HE would tell me where to publish it.
Instead, before you is a book that HE gave me to share with you.

And just as FATHER does; a lot of the information HE had me to publish was new to me, and much of it was what HE taught me previously. So, much this information was new to me and it blessed me and sharpened me as well.

A lot of what is written may not be received by everyone, but I was obedient in serving what the LORD gave me to serve. HE'S the COOK and I'm just the waitress.

Anyhow, I pray that this information blesses your life and changes your life for the better. I know and believe that many souls will be delivered from this learning material. It's a matter of lifestyle change, but more than anything; it is a matter of faith.

Thank you again and GOD bless you.
Tiffany Kameni.
www.tiffanykameni.com
www.anointedfire.com

Table of Contents

Introduction

I wrote this book after a couple of dreams that I'd had. Each time, the LORD had me to get up and write. The first part that I actually wrote was a note to the women of GOD about the spirit of whoredom. The rest of the information was birthed in message form through another dream. Nevertheless, the spirit of whoredom chapter is the final chapter of this book.

The Spirit of Heaviness and All Its Cousins is a must-read, power-house of a book that will surely open eyes, bridge understandings and shed light on the mysteries of demonic oppression. This is one of those books that is mainly written for the mature Christian, since this book delves into the depths of demonology.

The reviews have been great and many have been reportedly set free after reading this book. Freedom starts first in the mind because demons enslave the thoughts of their prey to keep them in bondage. After a man's mind is bound, he doesn't have to be "possessed" by a demon anymore because he will repetitiously yield to whatever he has allowed into his mind or whatever has been deposited into his mind. Once a man's mind is free to dig into the WORD of GOD, he will learn to pick up the SWORD of GOD.

Anyhow, I hope that this book blesses you as it has done with so many others.

The Spirit of Heaviness and All Its Cousins

What is the spirit of heaviness? Is that its actual name? How can I get rid of it? There are so many questions about this spirit, since it has bound so many and caused them to err.

Heaviness is not its actual name. Heavy, slothful, depressed and worthless is the way that it makes its prey feel. The spirit of heaviness is also known as the spirit of depression. But, is that its actual name? No, because they are not the same. Depression is one of the symptoms, not just one of the spirits. So, what is its name? Answer: There are many, so they are called Legion. (Refer to Mark 5:9)

Legion is not always the mixing of the same types of spirits. Legion is a host of demons that come as an army to siege and overthrow GOD'S government in a person; which is the order of GOD and that person's ordained purpose. It is important that we know who and what attacks us so that we can arm ourselves by disarming the terrorists that live within us or places a siege around us. Who is that terrorist? Our flesh.

Before we go forward, you may be saying, "Well, when we are saved, we can't be possessed by a demon, since we are inhabited by the HOLY SPIRIT!" And you are right, but when a demon can't get on the inside, it stands guard on the outside. Let me explain.
A person that is possessed is just that, possessed. Meaning

that they can operate either as themselves or the parasite (demon) that lives within them can sometimes partially or fully operate their bodies; depending on the strength of that person at any given moment. Most of the time when we see a full-blown possession of demonic activity, it is during the time when that person is at his or her weakest. It's when they are going through something that is weighing down on their emotions. Emotions are simply the response of the flesh. In some cases, some people don't go through something, but they live in demon territory by refusing to forgive and obey GOD; therefore, you may find them always under attack.

When we are saved, sanctified, and filled with the HOLY GHOST, a demon cannot enter our spirit; but it can build a siege around our soul.

Satan's plan is to steal, kill and destroy. Satan's goals for the saved is to stop them from living the life promised to them by GOD. To do this, he must stop knowledge from coming in. This way, we don't operate in our purpose, but we operate against our purpose. You will always either be for what GOD said or against it. Knowledge's root word is "to know." Knowledge, in the biblical sense, means that you know what GOD has said and you know what you are supposed to be doing. But, Satan loves ignorance. Ignorance's root word is "to ignore." Meaning something or someone is present, but we choose to ignore it; even if it's for a season. We ignore the Truth and in doing so, we render ourselves ignorant. The Bible is present to be read and there are many church buildings standing where we can go and hear the WORD of GOD; but when we refuse to let the WORD in, we are in the same refusing to cast that devil out.

GOD said, "My people are destroyed for lack of knowledge: because you have rejected knowledge, I will also reject you, that you shall be no priest to me: because you have forgotten the law of your God, I will also forget your children." (Hosea 4:6)

Pay attention to what HE said. HE said that HIS people are destroyed for lack of knowledge! Not unsaved folks, but HIS own; people who proclaim to know HIM, yet their hearts are far from HIM.

This is how Satan kills the saved. By getting them to starve to death from the lack of knowledge. You can have a table covered with food, but if you sit there for a period of time and refuse to eat it, you will eventually starve to death. When we refuse to feast on knowledge, wisdom and understanding, we literally starve ourselves to death.

Another plaguing lack that Satan sends is the lack of understanding. That is, you may know what GOD says, but you do not understand it. Think of it this way. If you were living in China, and you did not speak Chinese; wouldn't you be in grave danger every day? Let's say you were freezing to death. The temperatures were below zero, and you were wearing a tank top, shorts and flip flops in China. Someone says to you every day, "到我家來，這樣你就不會凍死" (Translated: "Come into my house so you don't freeze to death!") However, you think they are yelling at you every day, so you show them your prized middle finger and continue to read your bible under the tree; waiting on one of those words in the bible to come out and cover you up. This would mean you lack understanding. You did not understand what the man was saying because you went into a place unprepared for the climate and the people. You don't speak Chinese, and you are not dressed properly for the climate; therefore, in such a situation, you would surely die.

This is how the lack of understanding works. I have met people who lacked understanding due to their ignoring or misinterpretation of Proverbs 3:5, which reads, "Trust in the LORD with all thine heart; and lean not unto thine own understanding."

They trust in themselves, not understanding that the flesh interprets according to the flesh. The flesh tries to make sense of what it does not understand. That is its nature, and the nature of a thing is the temporal state of a thing; but the spirit of a thing is its eternal state. Therefore, your temporal tries to reason with your eternal and this just does not work. The scriptures tell us to trust in the LORD with all, not some, of our hearts. This is to keep us from leaning to our own understandings. But, when we don't trust HIM fully, we rely on self to explain a thing, when self can't even explain how you woke up this morning. If I don't understand Chinese, I can't speak Chinese. If you don't understand the WORD, you can't speak the WORD; instead, you will speak some words that are powerless against the enemy. That's why you see some praying for hours on end; waiting on a breakthrough or the right words to set things in motion and stop all the commotion they've been experiencing, when all they needed was the WORD. *"But when you pray, use not vain repetitions, as the heathen do: for they think that they shall be heard for their much speaking." (Matthew 6:7)*

What other lack kills and destroys GOD'S children? "The lips of the righteous feed many: but fools die for lack of wisdom." (Proverbs 10:21) What is it to be righteous or just? *"But that no man is justified by the law in the sight of God, it is evident: for, **The just shall live by faith.**" (Galatians 3:11)*
There are many people who go to church every Sunday, but they are not righteous. How is that? They don't live by faith! What is faith? *"Now faith is the substance of things hoped for, the evidence of things not seen." (Hebrews 11:1)* To have faith, one must first have substance. Substance means to be filled. We have to be filled with the WORD of GOD. Remember, faith comes by hearing and hearing by the WORD of GOD. Faith must always show its evidence, otherwise, it's not faith. A good example is the rich man who came to JESUS. He had done everything right in his life. Did that make him righteous? No. What did JESUS say to him? *"Then Jesus beholding him loved him, and said unto him, **One thing** you **lack**: go your way, sell whatsoever you have, and give to the poor, and you shall have treasure in heaven: and come, take up the cross, and follow me." (Mark 10:21)*
And what happened next? Mark 10:22 reads, *"And he was sad at that saying, and went away grieved: for he had great possessions."* He trusted in his things and not GOD. He loved GOD and served HIM partially, but he loved his wealth more and we can't serve two gods.

What are these lacks? They are evidence of strongholds; siege spirits encamping around the soul of a man with the sole intention of destroying that man. It operates by keeping wisdom, knowledge and understanding from going in; therefore, keeping the true and uncompromising WORD of GOD from going out. Their intention is to break his spirit and render him powerless. When you siege the soul of a man, you will eventually drive his soul out. Please read 2 Kings 25:1-6:

"And it came to pass in the ninth year of his reign, in the tenth month, in the tenth day of the month; that Nebuchadnezzar king of Babylon came, he, and all his army, against Jerusalem, and encamped against it; and they built a siege wall against it round about. And the city was besieged unto the eleventh year of king Zedekiah. And on the ninth day of the fourth month the famine prevailed in the city, and there was no food for the people of the land. And the city was broken up, and all the men of war fled by night by the way of the gate between two walls, which is by the king's garden: (now the Chaldeans were against the city round about:) and the king went the way toward the plain.
And the army of the Chaldeans pursued after the king, and overtook him in the plains of Jericho: and all his army was scattered from him.
So they took the king, and brought him up to the king of Babylon to Riblah; and they pronounced judgment upon him."

Saints, that is EXACTLY how a siege works, even in the spirit realm! Remember, GOD uses the natural to explain the supernatural. A siege, in the natural sense, is designed to keep people from trading or tapping into the resources that keeps them alive. It also keeps them from leaving the boundaries of the city under siege. The plan is to keep food and living supplies from going in so that many of the residents would die from lack and the rest would be weakened; not able to put up much of a fight.

People can survive for years, in many lands, on what they grow from within. But, remember, everything grows according to its season; therefore, they will have to store up food and supplies in their time of plenty to supply their time of need. But, when people aren't busy, or in purpose; guess what they do? They breed. This is why in lands of lack, there are many hungry children and they keep multiplying. What else is there to do? As the mouths that need to be fed increases, supply decreases. After a while, a famine or lack takes full control and the people begin to eat whatever they can get their hands on; including their own children! Eventually, their soul is driven out of their body because what it needs is not coming in and demons are waiting to take it into captivity! Just as the rival kingdoms take the kings into captivity as he attempts to escape. They usually kill him or imprison him.

But, you say, "I'm saved! I can't be unsaved! Once I belong to GOD, I belong to HIM!" But, you have no faith? Did you know that without faith, you can NOT please HIM? What does JESUS say? *"I know your works, that you are neither cold nor hot: I would that you were cold or hot.*
*So then because **you are lukewarm**, and neither cold nor*

*hot, I will **spew you out of my mouth.**" (Revelation 3:15-16)*

HE spoke of your works! Remember, faith without works is dead! Dead means it's not alive; it doesn't exist!

A siege around the soul of a man is what causes heaviness in that person. A person under this attack will feel heavy, tired, slothful and depressed. They don't feel like reading the bible; they don't feel like praying or going to church, and they don't feel happy. They cry and complain a lot and do whatever they can to get back to their peaceful place. They remember the good times because the thoughts of these times are all that are left. They know there is something they need and are supposed to be doing, but they can't seem to bring themselves into doing it. Their finances go under attack and nothing seems to be coming in. They either have no money or not enough money because the need is there, but the supply is absent and they don't know what to do about it. In many of these cases, people begin to develop destructive habits like turning to food, gambling, drinking and so on for therapy. The purpose of the siege is to take their minds off of serving GOD and to bring their minds into a chaotic state that is only calmed by dependency. For example nicotine, alcohol, and drugs are chemicals sent in to put one's problems to sleep for a little while. Problem is, those problems wake up again and again until you eventually stop waking up altogether or until you get delivered.

A siege is simply a stronghold. It enables the flesh by disabling our lines of communication with GOD; thus rendering our purpose void. Depression is the presence of purpose coupled with the absence of action.

I remember having two beautiful dogs some years ago and they were not neutered or spayed. The female went into heat at six months old and I was advised by a breeder to not let the male breed with her while she was so young. She warned me that breeding her at such a young age would stunt her growth, and the children would probably be unhealthy or wouldn't survive their births. Because they were pure breeds, I did want to breed them eventually; but I didn't want my dog to have any problems, so I placed the male and the female in separate rooms from one another. My male dog scratched up the door in the room he was in, broke the window and howled all day. He knew she was in heat, so he scratched that door beyond recognition. He howled and cried, and nothing would soothe him. He knew that this was the time for him to breed; it was his instinct or natural purpose, and because he was being restrained from that purpose, he was restless. My female dog tried to find a way to run away so that she could fulfill her need to breed because they are animals, their purpose was wrapped up in the natural. We were given dominion over animals because we were made in our FATHER'S image. HE made us a little lower than angels; we are heavenly beings in earthly suits, but Satan wants us to put off our FATHER'S image and just be wild animals. That way, we'd be driven by instinct and not by the WORD of GOD.

So many people nowadays have given their lives to repetitive thinking and living, and they don't realize that their minds are under siege. Many don't understand what the people do in a city that's under siege. They simply do the same things over and over again; hoping that the siege will eventually lift. They give their thoughts to tradition and religious repetitions, and they are depressed because they are being withheld from their purpose. They are financially in famine because demonic spirits have built a siege around them. Sure, they go to church, but the siege or captivity still has them bound. Read the parable of the sower:

"And when many people were gathered together, and were come to him out of every city, he spoke by a parable: A sower went out to sow his seed: and as he sowed, some fell by the wayside; and it was trodden down, and the fowls of the air devoured it.

And some fell upon a rock; and as soon as it was sprung up, it withered away, because it lacked moisture. And some fell among thorns; and the thorns sprang up with it, and choked it.

And other fell on good ground, and sprang up, and bore fruit a hundredfold. And when he had said these things, he cried, He that has ears to hear, let him hear.

*<u>**And his disciples asked him, saying, What might this parable be?**</u>*

*And he said, Unto you it is given to know the mysteries of the kingdom of God: but to others in parables; that seeing they might not see, and hearing they might not understand. Now the parable is this: **The seed is the word of God.***

Those by the wayside are they that hear; then comes the devil, and takes away the word out of their hearts, lest they should believe and be saved.

Those on the rock are they, who, when they hear, receive the word with joy; and these have no root, who for awhile

believe, and in time of temptation fall away.
And that which fell among thorns are they, who, when
they have heard, go forth, and are choked with cares and
riches and pleasures of this life, and bring no fruit to
maturity."
(Luke 8:4-14) Now that we have determined what the
spirits of heaviness are; let us find out who is its relatives
and why are they visiting.

Legion's Favorite Cousins
-Spirit of Depression.
-Spirit of Perversion (Rebellion.) <Yes, this is one of the
legions that usually affiliates itself with this stronghold.>
-Spirit of Lust. (And its girlfriends 'jealousy' and 'envy.'
-Spirit of Gluttony and Greed.
-Anti-Christ Spirit.
-Spirit of Murder.
-Spirit of Poverty.
-Spirit of Offense.
-Spirit of Whoredom.

Spirit of Depression

The spirit of depression weighs and breaks a man's spirit.

"A merry heart doeth good like a medicine: but a broken spirit drieth the bones." (Proverbs 17:22)
The New Living Translation reads it this way, *"A cheerful heart is good medicine, but a broken spirit saps a person's strength."*

Have you been experiencing heaviness? Keep getting in trouble? How about your spouse or your teens? When there seems to be nothing to do, we tend to do the wrong things, but when we are engaged in purpose, we can't find time for idle thoughts.

How does one overcome this spirit? The answer to overcoming not just the spirit of depression, but all demonic spirits has always been in James 4:7, but so many people read it with religious eyes that they miss the message and just see the words. *"Submit yourselves therefore to God. Resist the devil, and he will flee from you."*

The answer is in authority. What is in control of your life? The answer should be who and that who should be CHRIST. When we allow HIM to reign over us, we are able to properly reign over what HE has given us.

Remember positioning. Our thoughts should not stand over us, but what is of GOD is law for our lives and what is not of GOD should be positioned under our feet. GOD explains the order in 2 Corinthians 10:4-6, *"(For the weapons of our warfare are not carnal, but mighty through*

God to the pulling down of strong holds;) casting down imaginations, and every high thing that exalteth itself against the knowledge of God, and bringing into captivity every thought to the obedience of Christ; And having in a readiness to revenge all disobedience, when your obedience is fulfilled."

GOD'S Order Is: Strongholds pulled down. Down means broken apart, scattered; not in the lead. Down means to be brought under submission; they honor what you say and not the other way around.

GOD'S Order Is: Down imaginations and every high thing that exalts itself against the knowledge of GOD. Down also means to arrest, to enslave; to place one's foot upon the neck, as to declare victory.

GOD'S Order Is: Thoughts must be brought into captivity, otherwise, they are free to come back. We cause them to submit by us obeying the LORD. Remember, *"Submit yourself to GOD and resist the devil and he will flee from you."* Don't be sin's slave, but instead be its master.

GOD'S Order Is: Put away carnal weapons, divorce the flesh and bind up devils. *"Verily I say unto you, Whatsoever ye shall bind on earth shall be bound in heaven: and whatsoever ye shall loose on earth shall be loosed in heaven." (Matthew 18:18)*

GOD'S Order Is: Readiness or preparedness. Armed for combat. When Abraham went to rescue Lot, he didn't go alone nor did he try to negotiate with his enemies. He prepared himself for battle and he took revenge and his nephew from the hands of the Mesopotamians. He brought

318 trained men and they attacked at night. (strategy)
He didn't run out of the bushes in mid day swinging and
screaming, "Give me back my nephew!"
He got himself in order and Satan cannot override order!!!

Spirit of Perversion

I know so many of you are reading to see what does the spirit of perversion have to do with this legion, and I know that many of you are thinking that perversion is anything and everything sexual, but it is not. Perversion means to "turn away from." When one is perverted, they have turned away from GOD'S order and began to follow another order. This is called disorder.

Of course, someone can be sexually perverted, but perversion comes as a whole, not in part. If they are sexually perverted, it is because they are just wholly perverted. They have turned away from the LORD in some part of their life and since we can't serve HIM partially, when we turn away, the whole man is perverted or separated from GOD. Think about Lot's wife. GOD said to Lot, his wife and children that they were not to look back, but she looked back and as a result, she turned into a pillar of salt. Why didn't her eyes just turn into a pillar of salt? Because we can't sin in part, when she sinned, the whole woman was guilty.

People that are perverted tend to not want to follow authority or the GOD arranged order of things. This includes a wife who refuses to submit to her husband or a husband who refuses to submit to CHRIST.

The Jezebel spirit is one of rebellion and disorder, for example. It comes in when the order that GOD has set in place is not followed, and the head is left uncovered and without protection for it. The head represents the authoritative figure or what leads us. This is because Satan is always trying to lead us, but GOD established an order so that we would be led by HIM and not directed by devils. The Jezebel spirit hates order. People with this spirit do not like to submit to anyone; they have to be in control, so they use all manners and devices to get this control. Perversion is just plain ole rebellion capped off by ignorance.

When one is sexually perverted, it is rooted in evil imaginations not brought into captivity, therefore, they take the man (or woman) into captivity. That is, the order that GOD established is not carried out in that person's life. Therefore, their thoughts rule them and their flesh submits to their thoughts.

A perverted child will disobey his or her parents because the GOD established order is not in place in their homes, therefore disorder and dysfunction takes authority over that home. Joshua spoke of this order in 24:15, *"And if it seem evil unto you to serve the LORD, choose you this day whom you will serve; whether the gods which your fathers served that were on the other side of the river, or the gods of the Amorites, in whose land you dwell: but as for me and my house, we will serve the LORD."*

The bible tells us that a disobedient child won't live half his days and we know this to be true. Look around you. Parents represent authority and anyone that is against authority is in rebellion. GOD teaches us so much about HIMSELF, as our FATHER, through the orderly setup of us learning and having to submit to our fathers and mothers. They teach us, feed us and correct us because they love us. GOD does the same.

The wages of sin is death so when a child decides not to honor the WORD of GOD, they are warring against GOD. It's the same way with us as adults. Sin entices us to use ourselves as portals of entry so that it can come in and deposit death. It wearies the mind and tempts the flesh; promising to give us the perverted desires of our hearts as a result of submitting to it. In other words, sin acts as a pimp; you do the work and it collects from you.

When people are perverted, nothing seems to go right in their lives; because they keep submitting to themselves, other people and demons. They refuse to submit to GOD, so they keep leaning on their own understandings, trying out different techniques, being manipulative and being offensive in an attempt to get their way. They go to work and try to rule over the office, even though they were not given the authority to do so; they go to church and try to lead the pastor, even though they are sitting in the congregation; they go into prayer and try to rule the LORD, even though HE is GOD alone. Wives go home and try to rule over their husbands, believing him to be an incompetent leader; men go after vain things and blaze their own paths because they believe that JESUS isn't the only way; people in kingdoms conspire to kill the king because they lust after his throne. (Read my article on perversion in the February edition of Anointed Fire Magazine by following this link: http://anointedfire.co/#/tiffany-kameni-february-2012/4560616950)

Spirit of Lust

Lust is not always sexually related. Lust means to have an ungodly desire for something or someone. If one desires to sleep with her husband, it is not lust; but if this same man was not her husband, it is lust because it is against the order of GOD.

If a man desires to buy shoes that are in a store, it is not sin; but if he desires the shoes on another man's feet, it is lust because he is coveting. If a man who is in ministry walks into another man's church and decides that he is sent to eventually take over this man's church, believing himself to be a David and this man to be a Saul; he is in sin because he is being driven by envy.

The difference between coveting and envying is the following: to covet is to desire and feel entitled to the things, but envy is to covet or feel entitled to someone's life.

"And he said unto them, Take heed, and beware of covetousness: for a man's life consists not in the abundance of the things which he possesses." (Luke 12:15)

Jealousy can be righteous or unrighteous. GOD has the right to be jealous about us, and a man has the right to be jealous about his wife. To be jealous is to be angry or envious about what is supposed to be yours or in submission to you, however, it becomes unrighteous when we desire things and people to be under us when they are not supposed to be. Lust is one of the pulls and draws of the Jezebel spirit. It uses lust, both sexual and non sexual to get its way. Lust is self manipulation or self deception. When people are under siege, they convince themselves that they should have something or someone because they are entitled to it; in their own enslaved minds. That's why a man who stalks his ex or a woman who stalks her ex is extremely dangerous. They believe that this person is their possession and no one else is entitled to them. Even if GOD did not call that person to be their spouse, they feel that they have paid for the life of the individual with time, money, sex and so on. Because the person that is being stalked formed a soul tie with the stalker, they usually have to go to desperate measures to rid their lives of these characters. A stalker was and is a stalker before he or she is hurt; their pain simply activates what is in them.

Note: (A soul tie is a demonic stronghold when GOD is not in the midst. HE has to be the third fold in the cord, otherwise, it's simply a heavy burden; an enslaving lust that seems to burn like starvation with no other means of satisfaction. Their need seems unquenchable and their pain seems unbearable. They play out thoughts of being together in their minds, convince themselves that it will happen, and activate their craziness when the object of their affections reject them.)

If someone is lusting after you: they have an ungodly desire for you and in some cases, it's not just in a sexual way. In some cases, there is something on your life that they are drawn to. A controlling and manipulative person, for example, has no trouble finding people that he or she can control. In many cases, it is your anointing that attracts people to you.

Think about this: A man goes to work and stays there 30 years, but he is lazy and doesn't do more than he's asked to do; sometimes, even refusing to do what he is required to do. Another man comes in and after working there two years, is promoted to the senior employee's manager. Mr. 30 years gets angry because he believed seniority was the order, when even the LORD doesn't go by seniority. He looks at the heart and the works! Therefore, the senior employee was wrong to believe that laziness coupled with seniority would elevate him. Remember, lust dies in our lives when Love lives in it!

Spirit of Gluttony

Ever notice how when you were depressed, you ate everything, but the dog, and even he was scared? Lust feeds the flesh and so does gluttony.

Remember, Satan's desire is to get you to allow your flesh to lead you; since your flesh can only lead to death. He wants you to put away the WORD of GOD and just be an animal; eat, breed, sleep and die. That's Satan's desire for you.

Gluttony is depression suppressed by excessive food intake. Gluttony, of course, brings on extra weight and extra weight encourages slothfulness. Slothfulness engages poverty and poverty has death on speed dial.

To a glutton, food is the answer. Gluttons procrastinate on doing what is to be done by suppressing the thoughts of doing it. It stresses them out to think about it, but a lot of food and a little TV helps them to put those thoughts to bed for a while.

Gluttons don't like to confront the issues in their lives. Everything is locked away and tuned out with food. Gluttony is greed, just with food.

To be greedy means to have the belly of hell. A greedy person is never satisfied, even though they believe that a little more should quench their hunger.

The spirit of greed is married to the spirit of envy. One never comes without the other. A greedy man always desires more; including the wealth, things, wife and children of another man. He can have his own wealth, things, wife and children; but he is enticed by the idea of having more. A greedy woman always desires more and nothing seems to be enough for her. She desires the wealth, beauty, husband and children of another woman.

We refer to a sexually greedy woman as a whore; which is short for whoremonger. We'll get to what a whoremonger is a little further into this booklet.

In truth, a woman who serves her body to more than one man is a whoremonger and a man who serves his spirit to more than one god is a whore, but a man who cheats on his wife is not a whore, he is an adulterer; since the crime was against his wife and his flesh. The bible says he committed adultery against his wife, and fornication is a sin against the flesh, and of course; these are sins against GOD, but the authoritative order is not challenged.

Think about unwise parents who are wealthy. They parent their children by giving them what they want because they believe money is the answer and the solution to all things. In many of these cases, where a child was led by money and disciplined by money; the child grows to hate their parents because what they really needed: discipline, love, wisdom, knowledge, understanding and work was not given to them. Instead, they got the flowers without the rain. How can they appreciate its beauty when they've never seen bare ground? Therefore, the children begin to think that happiness is in wealth, but the problem in their view is that the wealth belongs to their miserable parents. The only way they can get their hands on all of it at once (greed) is to snuff them out (murder.) This tells us that greed comes in when order is out of place.

Beware of suppressors. Some examples of suppressors include: food, video games, excessive working, medications, associations, etc. They are indicators that you are trying to drown out the noise coming from within. Purpose suppressed equals people oppressed and depressed.

Anti-Christ Spirit

An anti-Christ spirit is simply what it says it is. Anti means "against," which means that this spirit is against CHRIST. Funny thing is, demons know that CHRIST exists. They know that HE died for us and rose on the third day. They know HE is the Holy One of GOD. They know HE is the Truth and the Life and no man comes to the FATHER except through HIM. They know this, but they don't want you to know it because that means they have a right to your soul, should you not submit it to GOD.

If Burger King knew McDonald's hamburgers were cheaper and tastier (not saying that they are, that's a matter of opinion), would they would tell you that? Of course not. GOD wants you to live forever with HIM and Satan wants you to die forever with him; so the devil competes with GOD for your soul. He's not going to advertise the LORD and the benefits of serving HIM. If he can convince you that JESUS did not exist or never came, his campaign ads have paid off! Just wait until after the election! That's why the anti-Christ spirit begins to reason with the senses of a man or better yet, his understanding. It knows that we understand things naturally, but spiritually, what is given to us has to be given by GOD. So, we have to trust that GOD delivers to us what we need to survive; not only in our life here on earth, but in our eternal life. This means that we need faith to inherit the blessings of GOD, but curses await the doubtful.

The serpent came into the Garden of Eden and told Eve that

she, and her husband would be like gods if they ate of the tree that GOD commanded them not to eat from because that serpent was against the WORD. Eve looked from a natural place and lusted after the fruit of the tree and finally gave in. She wasn't even supposed to touch it, but she did and death was found in not the fruit, but in sin. And we know the rest. JESUS is the living WORD! And who is not for HIM is against HIM! Therefore, Eve was seduced by the belief that she could become equal to GOD. The lust to be a god drove her into the arms of death. She allowed a few words to make her dissatisfied with who she was, and made her lust after who she could become.

When a person is not allowing the WORD to come into their hearing, they begin to accept another report because we are like gas tanks; we must run on something, even if it's just fumes. And that's when they begin to search for what makes sense to their personal "right now," where they are, instead of trying to be changed. A person that doesn't want change, changes his associations. There are people who come to church, read their bibles and even minister to others, yet they still allow their ear and eye gates to take in demonic words and activities. They are still listening to evil music; still singing those words into their lives; still watching evil movies including sexually perverted movies; and still hanging around people GOD told them to get away from. And they are always under attack and saying that the devil is attacking them when in reality, sin simply came to claim what death has ticketed. Sin wants to deliver its wages to them and they don't want these wages, because it does not match what Satan said he would pay them for their double mindedness.

An anti-Christ is a lying spirit that is more than just a spirit. It is a principality, meaning it "rules over" or is the principle authority demon. People with an anti-Christ spirit are usually passionate about spreading what they believe because a principality is never satisfied with ruling over one soul; it desires governments and kingdoms, therefore it has its host to spread its message. They teach their doctrine to anyone that will listen and they'll often try to kill anyone that stands in their way.

Spirit of Murder

We should all know that murder and envy are twins. When Cain killed Abel, it was because of envy. GOD favored Abel and his offering, but HE did not look upon Cain and his offering with favor because of the wickedness in Cain's heart.

Envy says, "I want to be you or I want to have you." Often times people murder who they envy. Envy looks for people with the favor of GOD on their lives and when it finds them, it seeks to destroy them. Satan often uses characters that are within our same setting to pit up against us with envy. For example, in the church; Satan uses Christians to attack Christians because they are within their reach. Almost every religious scandal that broke through the news was played and repeated by people who proclaimed CHRIST; the world usually shakes their head and turns the channel, but many in the church will make a bigger spectacle of the fallen leader. When someone of the world falls down, the world drowns its own, but when someone of the church falls down, they are drowned by church folks.

As you can see, there is a difference between a Christian and a religious person. Religious people often harbor the same spirits as the Sadducees and Pharisees. Sadducees and Pharisees followed the law of the first Adam and even in that, they were hypocrites. Sadducees and Pharisees were murderers, killing any and everyone who would not submit to tradition. They were and are of the anti-Christ spirit! This spirit intimidates and murders anyone who is for CHRIST. Violence covers the lips of souls bound by a murderous spirit. Have you ever spoke to someone about what the LORD has shown you and they disagree? You continue to speak what GOD has spoken; refusing to submit to the words they are speaking, and they get mad and begin to speak death over you? In most cases, they don't speak it directly, but they hide their words behind scriptures; combining them with fleshly understanding to scare you into submission? You just witnessed the spirit of murder. It says "submit or die".

I had a friend who went to a church, and GOD warned her beforehand not to let the pastor of that church lay hands on her. She went there because she was hired to take this pastor's photographs, and the session was supposed to begin before service started, but the woman was late. So, she had to sit in the church; waiting on it to end so she could start the session. While in service, the woman (pastor) approached her and asked to pray over her, and she declined. The woman was insistent and grew more agitated with each decline. Finally, the woman screamed that she saw death on her. That spirit grew more and more enraged at her for declining prayer.

To kill the man, you must first assassinate his purpose. We don't want to just know of this spirit in the sense of killing the body; we need to know about it in whole because some murders don't start from the outside; they occur from the inside. For example, the LORD may tell you something. You know HIS voice; you know HE told you. You tried the spirit and it was of GOD! But, you share it with a friend and first thing out of his or her mouth is, "Well, that's not true. You have to remember that in Ephesians 6...blah blah blah." And you notice this friend does this ALL the time, you are never right. They try to lead you to believe that you need them for understanding because you are hearing from your flesh, and you don't understand anything. You are just a baby. You're never old enough to teach. You write what the LORD tells you to write, and they sit in as teachers, grading papers, telling you what think is wrong and what they think is right. Because they do not understand that we can be leaders that are truly sent by GOD; but what is being taught to the person they thought was their student is a seed or understanding that has not begun to yield its fruit in their life as of yet. Which means, even though they may have come into salvation a lot later than the leader did; they are older than the one who self erected him or herself as their teacher! People don't like the Truth, but that doesn't mean we shouldn't serve it. I can go to college for forty-four years and tutor a new student, but if I never graduate, that student may grow up one day and be my teacher; simply because I did not apply what I was taught. Faith moves continually, but doubt is heavy and doesn't like to move out of fear of failure.

Two people can both read the bible and GOD may give one an understanding of all of Revelation, but because of where the other person is, HE may hold back full understanding. Why? Because rebellion is a crime of a baby, which means some of what is written in Revelation and throughout the Bible may be too rich for him or her right now. One man's season of reaping understanding is another man's season of sowing questions. When these two characters associate or communicate outside of what GOD intended their communication to be, it becomes evil communication. When a baby and an adult tries to have a conversation; the baby insists, cries and whines that he or she is right. A baby will throw tantrums and be relentless in his or her pursuit to have his or her way and an adult, who has adopted this baby, may begin to look for somewhere to put this child up for adoption. Whoever wants the child can have the child; even the video game. (Parents-ouch moment.) The LORD called you to lead, but you tried to walk with the person you were supposed to be leading. And that's why GOD comes between the friendship and HE sends someone else to impregnate the seed you were supposed to fertilize.

This is why so many leaders who get too personal with the sheep ends up losing them. They are so busy withdrawing, trying not to offend their friend that they have forgotten their purpose in his or her life all along. After all, in associating with them; they have found that the baby is agitated very easily, so they withdraw from giving them the whole WORD of GOD. They even begin to dilute the WORD with flesh; saying things like, "GOD said fornicators can't enter heaven! But, I remember when I was a fornicator. His name was _____. Anyway, _____ used to pick me up and take me to the motel behind the big hotel, and we would carry on into the wee hours."

What happened in this conversation? The leader had to backslide in thought and talk just to relate to the baby. In these relationships, the baby doesn't grow; the leader just becomes more childlike and in doing so, they are killing babies. Any child that is not fed will starve to death!

Murder isn't just the killing of the body; it is the killing of purpose.

Spirit of Poverty

Poverty means to lack a needed thing: be it food, shelter, water or the WORD. Poverty is lack manifested. Slothfulness is poverty's strong man and procrastination is poverty's strong man.

Let me share with you how the spirit of poverty works. It is even upon some rich folks! When money comes in; it's like having a mouse in your house, you won't rest until it's gone.

Around tax season, the LORD started ministering to me about poverty and what it is. I saw people anxiously awaiting refunds, and even though they were waiting for the manifestation of the money, they'd already spent most or all of it in their heads.

No matter where I worked, it was the same rotation every year. You'd see people who lived in lack all year: who depended on the government to sustain their homes and provide food for them, all of a sudden come into five to ten thousand dollars, sometimes more. Before you know it, the latest vehicle is pulling into the work parking lot; the clothing stores are being emptied out; TVs are on back order and so on. People look really good around January to April, but, in most cases, the money is gone within a month or a lot less and the repo man is outside their homes by September.

People of poverty spend whereas people of prosperity invest.

Poverty looks for a quick scheme to get rich. Maybe a fall inside a local Wal-Mart, a trip to the casino, or a lottery ticket begins to sound enticing to them. Money is not allowed in their home; it has to go, but it is hunted to extinction in their walk. Nevertheless, anytime they get their hands on any extra cash, they spend it frivolously.

Poverty lives for the moment. I was under siege by this spirit at one point in my life. What happens is, the heart begins to play these thoughts of new clothes and fun, and you can have it right now! Because you got the money to do it. Go and get yourself some new clothes, new furniture, a new car and so on. Poverty wants to get that money out of your hand and fast! In poverty, one lives for the moment because it feels good to sit in the mall eating and knowing that your purse has a couple of thousands in it ready to be spent. It feels good to break open those boxes and nail the new wall art to the wall. It feels good to pull up in your new car. It feels good to sit in a restaurant; not worrying about the price, being able to treat our friends and family and to give the waitress more than a $3 tip. Yes, that feels awesome!

But, what happens when the money is gone? The smoke clears and oppression, recession and depression all together say, "My turn". And these are long term states which are widely accepted for a moment of or a sense of prosperity.

A man of prosperity invests his money. He may establish a trust, buy property, or start a business. Now all these references to "he" means both men and women, so don't get lost in the words. A man of prosperity sacrifices the short term for the benefit of long term gain, but a man of poverty sacrifices the long term for the pleasures of a short term sense of prosperity.

Let's say, someone that got a large tax refund back had been delivered from the spirit of poverty. They got back ten thousand dollars and put it in the bank. Sure, she needs new clothes and her car is a little out of date; sure, she's pulling up to work in a 2001, while her co-workers are pulling up in 2010s or higher; sure, she's not out getting her hair done every week and her nails done every time they peel, but she isn't focused on her today; she's focused on her tomorrow. Therefore, she may go out and buy an acre of land and put the rest up for a rainy day.

All of a sudden, one day, that little acre she bought for $8,000 has tripled in value! The housing market did just that within the last few years. Now, let's say that she decides to sell this land and buy three lots in a place where the housing market has been a little slow. A few years later, that $24,000 is valued at $72,000, not to mention she picked up the valuable knowledge of property sales and purchasing. She takes that knowledge and writes a book which becomes a best-seller. She continued to live in faith, knowing that GOD would sustain her. I have literally seen people unemployed, buying cars from the "surprise" money that GOD sent to them. I have seen people who have been laid off or fired buying homes! I have seen them sit at home without a worry to their name and live better than people who work full time! Because even though they lacked a job, they did not lack what was vital to their existence; faith!

A lot of people won't be able to receive what I'm about to

say, but many will. Religious people think they need a job to survive, but the righteous know they need only to work to survive. They are not one in the same.

A job is a place of employment, working under the lead and authority of another person. Work implies purpose. A person can work fully in their heavenly purpose and make more money doing the will and work of GOD than a person at an office being disrespected, mistreated and ridiculed.

But, to graduate from job to work, one must first understand the difference between the two and TRUST IN THE LORD. To get full-time income from home, you can't have part-time faith. Now, that doesn't mean that you should go out and quit your jobs. That means you should ask the LORD to lead you to purpose and to supply your every need. HE already said HE would give you the desires of your heart! GOD called us the head and not the tail; we come behind in no good thing, but poverty puts you at the tail of worry.

Give a man of prosperity the lack in which a man of poverty has and he will turn it into prosperity. Give a man of lack everything that a man of prosperity has and he will turn it into poverty. Let's take it a step further: Give a man of lack everything five men of prosperity has and he will turn it into poverty. How is that? A man of prosperity will invest and use the resources around him. He has knowledge and he searches for more knowledge. A man of poverty will spend everything he has and the lender's money, hoping that somewhere, somehow, more money will come along.

Poverty loves people who don't operate in purpose or know their purpose. I remember how poverty sent many birds of prey after me when I first got into designing and all of the things the LORD has me doing. I had people telling me that I was in the wrong: seals and logos were basically evil; I didn't know how to design, and my favorite; I needed to go out and get a job. Needless to say, I disassociated myself from these people because their words did not match what GOD told me.

Since then, I have done well in my gifting and the LORD has sent me many people who desire to move into their purpose and activate their gifts. One thing that I found around each and every one of these characters were birds of prey: people who were telling them the wrong thing, driving them to the wrong place and justifying their poverty by telling them to keep on waiting on the LORD. HE will make a way. Did they not get the memo? JESUS is the Way, the Truth and the Life! And HE said in John 10:10, *"The thief comes not, but to steal, and to kill, and to destroy: I am come that they might have life, and that they might have it more abundantly."*

People like to ridicule prosperity preaching, but no one has anything to say about the poverty preaching; leaders living in lack inviting you into lack and telling you that this is the will of GOD for your life. Wasn't it the same GOD that we serve that supplied Abraham, Isaac, Solomon and Jacob with abundance? Did David suffer lack? Job was what we refer to as filthy rich.
We don't have to desire to be the richest of rich, but we should desire to be good men or women! *"A good man*

leaveth an inheritance to his children's children: and the wealth of the sinner is laid up for the just." (Proverbs 13:22)

Beware that you don't eat from poverty's table. Because what comes in us, always has to come back out.

Spirit of Offense

In sports, offensive players usually guard whichever teammate is holding the ball. Defense is when the team tries to stop the opponent from scoring, but offense is to disable the other team's defense so that your team can score.

What is the spirit of offense as it relates to our lives? Offense guards the demons that are in a man or encamping a man so that it may continue to score in that man's life. A man is a fool when wisdom is lacking; a man is a fool when knowledge is lacking, and a man is a fool when understanding is absent. *"How long, you simple ones, will you love simplicity? And the scoffers delight in their scoffing, and fools hate knowledge?" (Proverbs 1:22)* People usually reject what is familiar to them. When change is introduced to a fool, the spirit of offense comes to stand guard of what it considers its ball. It's been kicking him around for years and here you come with the truth?

In the same token, there is defense. When you know the WORD of GOD, people who lack that knowledge, but have adopted false doctrine will try to introduce it to you as truth, and a righteous anger may arise, but wisdom has to lead you out of that conversation. You can't convince someone that their way is wrong, especially when it's grafted in religiously.

You may see people defend their way of thinking to stop the Truth from scoring in their life. After all, that would reveal that they have been living as a loser and who's flesh can handle this reality?

And you may see people defend the Truth because someone is trying to introduce their understanding or perception (self deception) into their lives, in an effort to uproot the Truth.

One test that ALWAYS shows me that someone is operating in demonic purpose or are driven by the flesh is when I tell them that I'm doing what GOD told me to do or I've given it to GOD. When I hear, "Are you sure GOD told you that" or "GOD may be answering you through me," and I clearly know my FATHER'S voice and the voice of a stranger, I will not follow, I know it's time to rebuke and disengage.

I say this to keep a religious man from reading this and feel justified in his behavior of trying to change someone he thought needed to be changed; when really, he is the repetitious worshiper who may need a change in his church (building) and to stop reading the same scriptures over and over again, and disregarding the rest. Yes, people do this. They quote the same scriptures in 2012 that they were quoting in 1973. But if you corner them with the WORD, their last resort of offense is to say, "Well, man wrote the bible." That means, they have nothing left to say and offense is taking its position.

Heaviness always hires offense as its security. Before you reach the king, you must first go through his army.

I'll say this. If I allowed offense to drive me; I would be working in somebody's office building, living from paycheck to paycheck, probably unmarried, off somewhere fornicating, complaining, medicated, drunk and encamped around with a lot of evil association. Because people get offended when you don't change your life the way they think you should. Am I lying?

I can't tell you how many people came into my life and tried to uproot the WORD in my life and then got offended because I wouldn't allow them to do so; but instead, I repositioned them out of my life as the LORD led me to do. People try to score friendships with you, but first, some things about you has to be changed or moved around so they would feel comfortable with you. So, you get calls that sound like, "You hurt my feelings." Feelings are flesh, kill them.

We have to speak in authority otherwise, we justify offense. All too often people avoid sensitive subjects, because sensitivity means the wound hasn't healed and if we rub up against it, the person will react. That's what offense does. When you rub up against a lie with the Truth, Satan knows that person just might get healed. And that's when he sends forth his security: offense and defense.

Deliverance

Before we go into the teaching about the spirit of whoredom, let me share this with you. To get delivered from these spirits, you must first go after the principal demon, or principality. If an army sieges a land and that army is killed, chances are that king has more army men to send against you. He sent a portion, but believe me, he didn't send his strongest on the first go.

For you, Satan may send your friends to try to change your mind. When that doesn't work, he raises your family up against you, challenges you in the workplace, and tries to overthrow your sanity. Your children may begin to act disrespectfully, your spouse may begin to act disrespectfully or you may get challenged on every side.

An attack, in Satan's eyes is designed to bring you down. But, GOD allows these attacks for the sole purpose of building up your faith and your strength. You see, when you know you can survive a thing, then you will.

Take into account how when many of you were growing up, how poor you were. Nevertheless, you still ate good. No matter how hungry you got, food came from somewhere, even if it was just a ketchup sandwich or a piece of sugar toast, you ate. And you were happy and didn't know you were poor. On the flip side, many were born into wealth and when that wealth was threatened, they took their life. Why? Satan convinced them that they could not live without that wealth, but he can't convince someone that's been poor that they can't survive without wealth because they already have. In essence, Satan will lie to you, but when Truth is already in place in your life, every lie thrown at you will be rejected.

People often stay in siege worrying about what people are going to think about them or say about them. But, this is what the LORD told me. When a person speaks over your life, they did not lie. What they have spoken has the right to come and try to take its place in your life, but you were created in will. That means you have to receive or reject it. When they spoke it, they simply gave an evil report. But, it is what you do with what is said that will determine if that thing manifests in your life or not! If someone called you broke, then lack would seek you out. But, if you turn and speak what GOD has spoken, you are rejecting their words, and their words have to return to them and declare them a liar and liars are already judged!

Job did not receive what his friends were trying to speak over him because he knew that they spoke out of ignorance. Had he received it, it would have become reality for his life and he would in turn be saying to the LORD that he did not believe or receive what GOD has said.

When the doctor says you are sick, you are to rebuke the words and reject them. You say, "No offense doctor, but Isaiah 53:5 says 'But he was wounded for our transgressions, he was bruised for our iniquities: the chastisement of our peace was upon him; and with his stripes we are healed.' So, you may say what you see, but I say what I know, and because I know I am healed, whatever is trying to invade my body has been rejected and must now go away from me."

Ever wonder why a man went to the doctor, only to be told that he has had cancer at least for 10 years, but one month after being told this, he dies? Because cancer or infirmity placed him under siege, but once he received that report, cancer came in and had the right to operate in the way he believed it would. He had faith cancer would kill him and faith is designed to deliver.

To be delivered, we must deliver ourselves wholly to GOD. Get into purpose and get all of those people out of your ear gates who keep telling you something different than what GOD has told you. If you believe people do not affect change in your life, you are wrong. Evil communication ruins useful habits. There are so many people who are brought down by their associations.

I tell people every day. If a friend is speaking in an unfriendly way, then what is in their heart is being made manifest. You either choose to allow them more time to bring you down, or you move forward and keep them lifted in prayer.

We want to get delivered from Satan and his demons, yet, you harbor demonic friendships. Everything is purposed in birthing something and if someone is trying to impregnate you with a lie, eventually you will conceive that thing and give birth to more lies. I see people holding onto friendships that GOD delivered them from long ago, but they stay because their friend is Christian. What they didn't know was while David was king, his own son, Adonijah, declared himself king and sought out to kill his own dad. Even lay with his wives! However, what GOD said over David's life stood. David was king. Eventually, Adonijah and his evil council were killed.

Sometimes people declare themselves Christians, but what you didn't know was they were lukewarm and got spit out long ago. Howbeit, they keep trying to head up your life, all the while fornicating, gossiping and speaking evil of their Christian brethren, and you keep holding on thinking they'll change. If a man won't change for the LORD, who are you that they will honor your presence?

Deliverance starts in obedience. You can't have one without the other. It's that simple. You want to be delivered? Obey the WORD of GOD. You want to obey the WORD? You have to know the WORD. You want to know the WORD? You must hear the WORD. You want to hear the WORD? Read it and go to whatever assembly GOD sends you to get it.

You may be asking, "Why is she talking about deliverance before she talks on the last spirit mentioned? The spirit of whoredom, that is." Because I wrote up something a while ago on the spirit of whoredom and I am going to include that writing in this booklet.

Steps to Deliverance

1. Get rid of false doctrine. Read your bible everyday and ALWAYS ask the LORD for understanding. 2. Disassociate from evil communication and communicators. Pray about your leader. GOD told me that whatever is wrong with the head will affect the body. That is, if you walk into the wrong church, the wrong things are going to follow you out of it.

3. Don't go to a church because your great granddad and 3 generations of your men went there for more than a century. Could that be why you guys keep battling the same ole demons? Or could it be that back then, that place was holy, but now, it's under evil leadership?

4. Protect your ear gates. Stop listening to gossip, slander and music that exalts itself against GOD. If the guy is singing that he wants to make love to a woman that is not his wife, it is EVIL COMMUNICATION. If the woman is singing about her body, it is EVIL COMMUNICATION. If the song is violent, it is evil. To be accepted by GOD, the words must match what HE says. Otherwise, you are taking in lies, demons and evil reports.

5. Protect your eye gates. Sure, scary movies were the thing at one point, but didn't GOD tell you that HE did not give you a spirit of fear? So, why are you entertaining movies obviously put together by demons who are trying to instill fear in the audience or viewer?

Why are you watching porn?

6. Pray every day. Not religious prayers, but talk to FATHER. Tell HIM how you feel and ask HIM for

deliverance. (Ye have not because ye ask not.)

7. Read your bible every day. When the WORD moves in, lies are evicted.

8. Praise GOD every day. The devil hates praise. The quickest way to get him to flee is to obey GOD and praise GOD.

9. Obey GOD every day. Make up your mind today that you do not belong to you therefore, you can't let you rule over you. You belong to GOD.

10. Keep living.

Living Right- Living Righteous

First thing you need to be aware of is any demon sent out will try to come back.
Luke 11:24-26 reads:
"When the unclean spirit is gone out of a man, he walks through dry places, seeking rest; and finding none, he says, I will return unto my house from which I came out. And when he comes, he finds it swept and in order. Then he goes, and takes with him seven other spirits more wicked than himself; and they enter in, and dwell there: and the last state of that man is worse than the first."

We don't want this, right? So, we want to be sure that it doesn't come back and cannot come back. But, here is something I have learned. We, as believers are the head, the authoritative figure and we don't have to let it come back, neither do we have to give it an opportunity to return. So, let's exercise our Luke 16:19 rights: "And I will give unto you the keys of the kingdom of heaven: and whatsoever **you shall bind on earth shall be what has been bound in heaven**: and whatsoever you shall loose on earth shall be what has been loosed in heaven."
The key word here is "bind."

You have the right to bind it and cast it into the pit until the day of Judgment. Demons don't have earth suits, meaning they are illegal in the earth realm, so begin to bind it with your words. If you have a believer who can stand with you, even better. Now, don't mistake this. You can do it by yourself, but the WORD said: "For where two or three are gathered together in my name, there am I in the midst of them." (Matthew 18:20)

I usually do it alone because my faith is there, but if there is something that challenges you emotionally, it is better to have a gap stander that will stand in for you just in case your emotions get the best of you and cause you to doubt. You see, that devil can easily get the person it is attacking to doubt by simply attacking or enticing the believer's natural senses.

Let's say, for example, a believer lost her job. We'll call her Jasmine. Her bills are overdue and she doesn't know what to do, but she's believing GOD for a miracle, so she calls on her prayer partner Amber and asks her to stand in the gap with her. Amber does.

Whatever devil or stronghold is assigned to attack Jasmine is working overtime. It knows that Jasmine and Amber prayed, but it also knows that without faith or works, there will be no miracle manifestation. So, all of a sudden, Jasmine gets a call that Dad is in the hospital and when she rushes out to go and visit him, her car won't start. These things do happen. You think it's a coincidence?
Now, emotionally spent and overwhelmed, Jasmine begins to declare against what she prayed for. She starts saying and believing that she is going to lose her house, her dad isn't looking good and to top it off, they don't want to renew her teaching license. She calls Amber and just cries about what she believes is going to happen. That's one touchdown for that devil, but he hasn't won the game just yet. He now has to get Amber to doubt, but that isn't as

easy since Amber isn't directly affiliated with what Jasmine sees. So, he's going to have a hard time knocking Amber down and there is a big chance that he won't be able to do it.

Now, let's bring a third person into the mix as a prayer warrior. Amber called Mr. Jamison, her Uncle, who is a believer and asked him to stand in the gap for Jasmine as well. What just happened here?
"And if one prevails against him, two shall withstand him; and a threefold cord is not quickly broken." (Ecclesiastes 4:12)

Now, that devil might as well give it up because even against a stronghold or brigade of demons, two believers are an army!
Unity is vital in this hour. Do you know how powerful it is?
"And the LORD said, Behold, the people are one, and they have all one language; and this they begin to do: and now **nothing will be restrained from them, which they have imagined to do.**" (Genesis 11:6)
Why do you think that your marriages, churches and Christian friendships are under attack? Because Satan likes to scatter the sheep.
Pay attention to how a wolf hunts. If a pack of wolves are chasing sheep, they will try to hide and sneak up on them and then scatter them. After that, they will chase after the slowest, smallest or weakest one, and they'll come back another day for another one using the same tactics.

If you want to live right, you must live and love righteously. That is, you must live by faith, and faith comes by hearing and hearing by the WORD of GOD.

Your Pastor may be great, but you can't put your burden on him or her when JESUS said to cast your burdens upon HIM.

Yes go to church, but get into that Bible EVERY DAY OF YOUR LIFE.

You can read a chapter a day, but be sure to pray for understanding first, since we understand things naturally and we don't receive what doesn't make sense to our natural man.

To change your life, you have to change your mind. That is why the WORD of GOD has to come in you in abundance so that what was in you will be evicted.

Make a list of the things you want changed about you and take them to GOD.

Now, do the works. Got a problem gossiping? Stop associating with gossipers and try blessing the person you feel inclined to gossip about by speaking good of them and not evil. Do you know that if a gossiper calls you and starts to tell you about Brother Blake and his alleged girlfriend and you say, "Well, I hope that's not the case and I will be praying for him. GOD is awesome and I know that GOD'S will for his life is that he live and be blessed. It's just a shame that people prefer to talk about him than to pray for him," you will shame the messenger. I know; I've done this plenty of times and what usually happens is they respond with, "Yeah, I will pray for him. You're right. Hold on. *(Talks in background)* Huh? Who? Hey, Tiff, I'll call you back." ***Click***

What happened? James 4:7 is what happened. "Submit

yourself to GOD and resist the devil and he will flee from you."

Also, lifestyle changes have to occur.
Again to change your life, you must change your mind. Introduce blessed thoughts to your mind. Write down, not what you want to have, but what you will have. Faith is not saying what you want, faith is saying what is mine. If I keep saying I want something, I'll keep on wanting, but if I say it is mine, I will have it in the season of harvest. Meaning, I may not get it that day because I just laid the seed, so I have to now go through the seasons of cultivating and waiting.

There is so much that you have to throw out and so much that you have to purchase with your faith.

Here are a few tips:

- Get rid of evil associations and communications. Communications is not just who you communicate with, it's who and what you allow to communicate to you and this includes music and TV shows that you may love to watch. Reality shows are funny, but do you really want this mess going into your ear and eye gates? Because demons use our minds to enter our hearts. Guard your heart, child of GOD. You don't open up the gates to let criminals in and then send security to tell them that they've went far enough. You don't let them in....period. Devils are thieves; remember that.

- Watch your mouth and rebuke yourself about what you are saying. Don't allow you to hinder you.

That is, keep your faith in your mouth and in your heart and don't allow any other reports that contradict who you are and Who you serve to escape your mouth, or better yet, enter your heart.

- Stop fornicating. You're praying, you're fasting, and you're fornicating? Even in the midst of your fornication, you are waiting on the LORD to bless you? Seriously? GOD still loves you and watches over you, but when you lay down with a person that is not your spouse, you lay down with their devils and since what you are doing is sin, you are lying down in the Devil's bed and giving the Devil rights to you, and then you fall under attack behind attack. Funny thing is, people sometimes get chastened for their wrongs and think they are under attack. No, you're getting a whooping. Learn from it and do better. JESUS said HE doesn't condemn you, just go away and sin no more.

- Stop committing adultery. How you treat your spouse will determine how GOD treats you.

- Get over yourself. Out of every relationship I have ever had to get over, this was the hardest. When we get over 'me,' we put offense out of a job.

- Ask the LORD to remove any and every one from your life that HE doesn't want in it and to position every one that is in your life in the place that HE wants them to be. Often times, we promote or demote people in our lives in places that GOD didn't call them to be, and then we wonder why we are causing friction with one another.

- Start new and good habits.

- Determine what it is that you want and start it today and refuse to go a day, (unless the LORD leads) not to work on what it is that you want. You say you want to make clothes? Go buy some fabric. You want to quit your job and start your own business eventually? Start studying for the business you want. There is much to learn. You say you want to be married? Learn how to cook and fix things. Pray that the LORD prepares you.

Procrastination

Fight this by just doing what you should and want to be doing. No more waiting. Because that's what procrastination makes you do. Wait, you say you don't have what you need to start? Do you not have Internet? Do some research and some writing. Get knowledge. You just don't understand how vital this is to your success. You have to move or do the works. Often times believers wait for their blessings to fall from the skies when real faith reaches for what is already there.

Relationships

Change how you talk to people and view people. We sometimes see people according to where we are and not who they really are. We look for intentions and motives when we should be looking for fruit. Our friendships won't grow until we do. Sometimes, as we grow, the LORD will remove certain friends from our lives for a reason and sometimes just a season, but a lot of times, the move is permanent. You have to be willing to let go, no matter how it makes you feel because GOD is removing them so you can both stop hindering one another. You may be an enabler or vice versa. They may be too common to you to receive from or deliver to you, therefore, your communications are always about the past when you were both dead in sin. This is evil communication and indicates that you have nothing to talk about, so you have to exhume the dead you so they can identify him or her again and again to keep their interest.

In your romantic relationship, you have to be married or marriage minded. You don't date someone for three years without ever having prayed for and about them.

Remember, it's easy to get married, but you got one in a 6 billion chance of marrying the right person, since there are more than 6 billion people reportedly on the earth. You think you can find her or be found by him by chance? You have a better chance winning the lottery 250 million times, but if you allow the LORD to be your compass, HE will always lead you to the one. I know that man who keeps eying you in the store is really cute, but wrinkles and a bad attitude later, he won't be worth it if he's not the one.

Your Children

If you don't get your children from this new video game obsession, then they will become a part of a straw generation. Satan will just pull whoever he wants to use for the day. I know we are busier and need something for our children to do, but why not make it productive? Get them to study the bible. Get them to write a weekly letter to an

orphan. Teach them to tithe. Teach them to be a blessing.
As parents, you have to get more active with your children
and stop letting video games and TV raise your children.
You got to stop letting your children disrespect you as well.
Get active.

Ministry
Get up, get out and do your part. There is no excuse for
you to sit on your gifts anymore. You think by waiting that
the day will come that you will feel like it? It'll never
happen because your flesh wars against your spirit. So, you
have to tell the flesh what it will be doing and not allow the
flesh to tell you what you will be doing. The flesh is dead
meat. Would you let a chicken wing tell you to eat dirt? If
it did, would you grab a spoon and scoop you up a dusty
treat? I hope not. Because that chicken wing is just a piece
of meat. Don't let meat speak to your spirit.

With ministry, always pray, as with everything. Make sure
you do what GOD tells you and when HE tells you. You
may begin to see something happening in the church
buildings and amongst the religious that troubles you (and
GOD), but HE is showing you for a reason. But, you are
going to have to obey HIM today and stop sitting on your
gifts. You never know when the Master is coming, so don't
be like the foolish virgins that JESUS told the parable
about, but be like the ones who took oil with them. That is,
be ready.
Even if you start online, just start. Even if you write some
prisoners, just start. (And if you are a single woman, unless
the LORD leads you otherwise, don't go pen paling with

male prisoners!) Pray about everyone. Even if you visit some orphanages, visit some nursing homes, cook extra food and drive around looking for the homeless to give them a meal, you are needed in this hour! Remember, it's not about you and how you feel, it's about saving lives. The harvest is plenty, but the laborers are few.

Finances

Oh, what a challenge for many. We, especially Americans, love to splurge and spend, but often times, we are so short sighted that we don't think about investing. You mean to tell me I have to wait a couple of years to see a return, but I can use this paycheck today and go and buy me some new shoes and a new X-Box? Poverty thinks short term and poverty thinks to spend, but you must determine if poverty is going to be your accountant another day. Our imaginations were designed to give us a window of insight into our future. We think how a thing is to be and it becomes because where our minds go, our hearts follow and when our hearts lead, we follow. It's common to think of what you wish you had and then turn around and believe for less. It's not GOD holding you back, it's you holding you back. Create for yourself good and blessed thoughts as to what you will have and write it down. Now, pray for it and claim it. No matter what you do or say, claim it every day, and write something about it every day. For example, you can say, I am going to go down to Florida in my new Mercedes. What you are doing is having an argument with your flesh and whatever devils that try to come against what you are believing for. Because your eyes see 'not enough', but your faith sees an overflow. You have to believe to receive, but in addition to that, we were created to receive and reject. We do this with our mouth. So receive the blessings and reject blessing blockers, and be sure to cancel evil words (yours and those that flow from the mouths of others) everyday. You don't know how many people are saying you want this, but you won't have that, and their words are coming to you looking to be received. Reject them so that they have to, in their life's form, go back and declare the sender a liar and carry back to them whatever sentence that tried to send upon you.

Lastly, be careful who you let in your ears. I know that there are many preachers who hate the prosperity gospel, but I want to share this with you. In truth, there are some devils that use this gospel to make their pockets fat, but there are some men and women who the LORD is using to teach you how to come out of your broke place, but because what Mr. Anti-Prosperity taught you, you don't receive the truth. And by the way, Mr. Anti-Prosperity needs to borrow $5 for gas. We can't adopt wisdom and false doctrine. I agree that if this man or woman's whole sermon is always about money, they may have a love for money. But, always pray and ask the LORD to lead you where HE wants you to go so that you won't end up under a head who is teaching you the wrong things.

Gifts/ Talents
It's simple. Stop sitting on them.
Do you know how many people I have met that were sitting on their gifts? Either because they believed they weren't ready to tap into them or someone was in their ear telling them that they weren't ready. My advice to them? The

parable of the talents. Keep goats out of your ears. Get busy and get into your gifts. Here is the parable of the talents:

"For the kingdom of heaven is as a man traveling into a far country, who called his own servants, and delivered unto them his goods. And unto one he gave five talents, to another two, and to another one; to every man according to his several ability; and straightway took his journey. Then he that had received the five talents went and traded with the same, and made them other five talents. And likewise he that had received two, he also gained other two. But he that had received one went and digged in the earth, and hid his lord's money. After a long time the lord of those servants cometh, and reckoneth with them. And so he that had received five talents came and brought other five talents, saying, Lord, thou deliveredst unto me five talents: behold, I have gained beside them five talents more. His lord said unto him, Well done, thou good and faithful servant: thou hast been faithful over a few things, I will make thee ruler over many things: enter thou into the joy of thy lord. He also that had received two talents came and said, Lord, thou deliveredst unto me two talents: behold, I have gained two other talents beside them. His lord said unto him, Well done, good and faithful servant; thou hast been faithful over a few things, I will make thee ruler over many things: enter thou into the joy of thy lord. Then he which had received the one talent came and said, Lord, I knew thee that thou art an hard man, reaping where thou hast not sown, and gathering where thou hast not strawed: And I was afraid, and went and hid thy talent in the earth: lo, there thou hast that is thine. His lord answered and said unto him, Thou wicked and slothful servant, thou knewest that I reap where I sowed not, and gather where I have not strawed: Thou oughtest therefore to have put my money to the exchangers, and then at my coming I should have received mine own with usury. Take therefore the talent from him, and give it unto him which hath ten talents. For unto every one that hath shall be given, and he shall have abundance: but from him that hath not shall be taken away even that which he hath. And cast ye the unprofitable servant into outer darkness: there shall be weeping and gnashing of teeth." (Matthew 25:14-29)

Spirit of Whoredom (A Note To The Women of GOD)

What is 'dis?' According to the World Dictionary, 'dis' is defined as "indicating negation, lack, or deprivation." In this article, you will come to understand what whoredom is, how it affects you and why you, as a Christian woman should disassociate yourself from whoredom.

Before one can understand whoredom from a carnal standpoint, one must visit it from a spiritual view. In reading the scriptures, the word 'whore' is mentioned 65 times in the unrevised King James bible. GOD referenced the word 'whore' in two ways, both budding from the same root; meaning to be unfaithful to the one you're supposed to be in submission to by whoring out your body or your spirit. On the spiritual side of it, FATHER warned the Israelites about whoring themselves to other gods, meaning they were defiling themselves and of course, being unfaithful to HIM. The penalty for such an act was to be given into slavery, war, death, etc. In this, GOD was 'putting away' or divorcing a generation and in many cases, several generations. Eventually, because of HIS undying love, HE would turn HIS wrath from them and reconcile them as a people unto HIM.

Now, on the carnal side of things, the world regards a 'whore' as a promiscuous woman. In addition, promiscuity is even defined individually; whereas some believe one to be promiscuous if they have slept with, at minimum, two men and others believe the number defining a woman as a whore begins at five or more men. But, how does GOD define it? Because, in truth, we are branded by what was spoken out of HIS mouth and the mouth of man is simply fading speech propped up on an evil heart, which means, it's not true.

We will visit this topic from the feminine side of it because, according to scripture, a whore;
carnally speaking, is a woman who has been defiled by a man who is not her husband. A man is only
referred to as a whore in relation to his worship of other gods. A man could, however, be labeled an
adulterer, which, by all means, is still unacceptable to GOD if he is married and goes so far as to even
lust after another woman.

Submission is simply to 'set under one's authority.'
CHRIST submits to GOD and man submits to
CHRIST. A wife submits to her husband and in this lineup, she too is submitting to GOD through her
submission to GOD'S order of things. When she prides herself out of line with the WORD of GOD and submits sexually to a man other than her husband, she is a 'whore.' Therefore, whoring is not just
sleeping with several different men; whoring is sleeping with 'any' man that is not your husband. Just
as the Israelites were called adulterers and whoremongers because they submitted to another god, a
woman is considered a whore when a man that is not her husband is allowed to carry out an act with

her that was reserved only for her husband. Sex.

Does this mean that a 'whore' has to be married to first be considered, in the eyes of GOD, to be a whore? No. Even a single woman, when she has sex with a man that is not her husband, spiritually and carnally speaking, she is considered a 'whoremonger.' I know this will put a squeeze on the pride of some because many, as a new generation of women have exalted themselves into a place of disorder. And this is where the 'dis' begin. Before we go on, keeping in mind, the truth bares its own light; meaning, it can be found in your bible, however, opinions and lies have no light because they stem from the heart of man. With that said, a man's act of adultery, in the contemporary sense, was not a crime 'against' his wife unless he put her away or divorced her and married another. However, if he married her and another woman, he was not guilty of adultery. Keep in mind that this was in a day that a woman was considered the 'property' of her husband, and property had little to no rights.

Nowadays, it is defined as adultery if he has intercourse with a person other than his wife, while he is yet still married. Simply put, GOD commanded husbands to honor their wives and to treat them as they treat their own bodies. GOD gave this commandment so that man would understand not only how to treat their wife, but the correct order or authority that a wife is to have in the home. This is proven in Sarah's request that

Abraham 'cast out' Hagar and Hagar's son with Abraham. Keeping in mind that Sarah sent Hagar, who was her maidservant, to sleep with Abraham and bear a child for Abraham, but after Sarah too had a child and saw Hagar's son mocking her son, she told Abraham to "cast her out" or send her away. Her request, quite understandably, was grievous to Abraham, but GOD told him to hearken unto the voice of his wife. That means to listen to his wife. As noted throughout the bible, a man was not considered to be 'out of line' in his decision to take several wives because of the laws and conditions of those times. Now, the law, before JESUS allowed a man to put away his wife by giving her a writing of divorcement. JESUS made it clear that the law was established by Moses because of the hardness of man's heart, but from the beginning, GOD'S law was that a man and his wife become one and divorce was simply not an option.

In accordance with the Old Testament law:

A man was only guilty of adultery 'against' a woman if he was to put her away or divorce her and marry another. (Mark 10:11)

A man could only be guilty of adultery against another man if he slept with that man's wife. At this time, such an act merited him being put to death along with the adulteress. But, if a married woman was caught in an act of adultery with a single man, only she would be put to death. Why is this? Because she was then defiled with the spirit of that man and now illegally his wife and as such, according to Old Testament law, could not be taken in by her husband again. To keep the land from being defiled by her and the wrath of GOD from coming upon that land because of her sin, she was taken outside the city and stoned. Now, much of the law, of course, was given by Moses, because of the people and their beliefs, but JESUS did away with that law, as evident in the story of the woman caught in the very act of adultery. (See John 8). JESUS rebuked the men who wanted to stone her and HIS command to her was to go away and sin no more.

Nowadays, the world has redefined 'whore' and because of this, many women feel justified in their promiscuous behavior. They believe that because they are not sleeping with a married man or more than 3 men, they are just women 'playing the game' of life. Nevertheless, when GOD commands an order to be carried out and it is not, disorder takes shape and an evil generation begins to arm itself against the LORD.

Where is the 'dis' list?
First off, of course, there is disorder. Thefreedictiorary.com defines disorder as: A lack of order or regular arrangement; confusion. 2. A breach of civic order or peace; a public disturbance. Now, medically speaking, the medical dictionary section defines disorder as: a derangement or abnormality of function; a morbid physical or mental state.
What happens is, when GOD'S order is not intact, what takes place is things get out of order, and because the order of GOD has been perverted in her life, she does not and cannot function normally

because a sane mind is a blessing from the LORD.
Therefore, she becomes distant, disturbed,
distrusting, disadvantaged, disconnected from truth,
diseased, disgraced, dishonest, etc. Men take her to bed
and then disassociate themselves from her and her children.
Her home is doomed to become one of dysfunction, if she
does not repent and turn from her wicked ways.

As a Christian woman, GOD does understand that we were
not always saved, but through the
purification of the BLOOD of JESUS, we can be saved and
set free. No more law to condemn us!
But, as a Christian woman, you should not be still enslaved
by the spirit of whoredom.
Whether you are married or single, there is only one
husband out there for you, but as in many cases,
many of us go into the church undelivered and leave
undelivered. Why? Is it our Pastor's fault? No,
deliverance does not knock at your door; you have to seek
it out and pursue it until you have it within
your heart's grips. That is, you have to repent and
repenting isn't just apologizing to GOD; repentance is
changing one's mind and turning it back to GOD.

Your flesh may burn with desire, but this is an issue of
death trying to weld up in you and this
has to be rebuked. Why bask in the pleasures of death and
then be surprised at the climax? This too
can be the evidence of the presence of demonic activity.
Therefore, you don't want to feed the desire,
you want to be delivered from whatever is heating you up

from within. And ladies, we do have to be
set free from past lovers because when we lay with a man,
we take in the spirit of that man, or
spiritually speaking, we become his wife....illegally. As
such, we cannot be taken by another man
to be his wife until we have been set free from the previous
lover. Now, I know, many women marry
anyway. This is one of the reasons that divorce rates are so
high. You have to understand that the spirit of the previous
man will war with the spirit of the new man. Scientists
have even found that when a woman has intercourse with
two men and both men release sperm into her, the sperm
wars with one another. This is why you don't have peace
from within. This is why you want to put a tracking device
on your husband's car when he attempts to go to the
supermarket. According to the scriptures, "the two shall be
one," and now, you've become one big mess.

It was not intended to be this way. Before you consider
marriage, you need to ask the LORD to deliver you from all
of your past lovers so that you can be found suitable for the
man of GOD that has reserved just for you. He cannot
come until you are set free. Others, however, will come.
You can go ahead and refer to them as your ex husband,
baby's father or the husband that is bringing you much grief
if you allow them into your life and into your bedroom.
Many women have also found and laid with what would
someday be their killer. This is sad, but true. Because
what is in the 'wrong' man is the right direction for his 'true'
wife, (only after he has matured carnally and spiritually)
and a 'wrong' way or disorder for any other woman who

attempts to sit down in his heart.

I can't tell you how many women I come in contact with on a weekly basis that are still bound by the spirit of an ex lover, and many of them are in ministry! This only happens when one is ordained before they are set free. Again, disorder takes place and now, a woman still bound is sent out to set others free. Of course, she cannot deliver what she does not herself possess, so the only delivery she is making is of demonic nature.

And she's not hard to spot. The evidence that she's still bound will show up in her talk and her walk. A woman bound will:

1. Talk of her ex and what he's done to her quite often.

2. Still be planning an assault, be it physical, spiritual or retaliatory against the man or men that have hurt her. She may look for ways to 'expose' or humiliate them.

3. Minister against men. Pay attention to her words. Do you hear the love of GOD or the contentions of an angry woman? Do not mistake her anger for strength. It's actually her weakness.

4. Have a distaste for men in leadership....therefore, she may prefer and ordain many women, but use men as helpers. She may also look for relationships from men that are not in leadership, even when she is. Why? Control. The submission has been perverted because she is perverted.

5. Have trouble in relationships. Her distrust for men creates a disturbance in every given relationship, so most men run in the direction of the first light of freedom.

6. Still wish the wrath of GOD to come upon the ex, rather than his deliverance. I have listened to many women, even YEARS after they've been victimized by a man still talk of and seek the day when GOD'S hand will come against him. This, of course, is the evidence that she is still bound by this man's spirit and has not forgiven him. She may say that she has forgiven him, but GOD said, "Look at the fruit!"

7. May feel the need to protect other women from a type of man or men, in general. She's always there, to lend a listening ear to your troubles with men and her recommended cure for trouble with one man is usually another man. She may also be all too ready and willing to go on the war front with any man she perceives to be hurting her friends. Why? Because, in her sight, he has the same markings of the man that hurt her.

What if this is you? How do you get set free from the spirit of whoredom, which breeds unforgiveness and a lot of unlisted physical and mental disorders? It may or may not be simple, depending on your seriousness with being set free.

1. One of the first things to do is to have a talk with GOD. You see, you cannot do this on your own. You need HIM.

2. Repent. That is, turn from the sin. Make up your mind to do differently. DO NOT PLACE YOURSELF IN SITUATIONS WHERE YOUR FLESH CAN SPEAK TO YOU. That is, don't be alone with a man, don't allow a man to pick you up, or convince you that your walk and talk alone will be a Christian one. If he truly wants you as his wife or is

considering you as a wife, he's not going to care where you are, as long as you are together.

3. Get rid of everything that the ex gave you. (Except the children.) Anything you keep has the power to rebind you. Sure, that diamond watch goes well with that diamond studded bag he bought, but get rid of them!

4. Next, fill yourself with the WORD of GOD regarding whoredom. You have to know what GOD says about this act before you can truly understand why it's wrong. Understand that the more WORD that comes in you, the more Satan is evicted from you.

5. Trample the devil with your praise! Feeling a little 'fiery' today? Get busy with praise. Get busy with worship. Don't sit around and let that stuff fester.

6. Avoid all men that give you that 'eye.' You know the 'eye of lust' when you see it. If you're not a virgin, you definitely know 'the look.' If you don't, it's a look where he seems to be extremely focused on you, passionate...a little out of touch with reality...kind of like a daydream. Now, it's a given...all men aren't the same, but 'the look' is unmistakable.

7. Submit to GOD and commit to GOD. Talk to HIM often and tell HIM what you are committing to HIM. You can do it. Believe me, the more WORD comes in you, the more you will commit to HIM because the fear of HIM will begin to override your lust and reclaim the places in you that was once under siege by the enemy.

Don't allow yourself to be disqualified as a daughter of the

Most HIGH just because your dead flesh is disputing with your spirit. GOD has given us a set of instructions and when we are disobedient, we cannot and should not expect to be rewarded. Your hump session will not yield a husband and if, by
chance, a man does marry you after having you his way, you better start putting on the full armor of GOD and quick! Because now, you're going to have to try to pray him into deliverance or pray to be delivered from him, and most times, it's the latter! A man of the flesh cannot and will not make an ideal husband. Instead, he will do fleshly things like, well...cheat, molest, sodomize, etc. *(P.S. Don't be fooled by titles....just because a man has a ministerial title does not mean he is not a man of the flesh. Everyone that claims to be of CHRIST is not.)*

Note: If you were considered a 'whore' before reading this article, you don't have to be one anymore. Today, praise GOD, pray to GOD, repent and declare yourself a woman after GOD'S own heart. Your
life can start over today. And please don't worry about hurting your ex-lover's feelings. GOD'S feelings is far more important than his, every day! Besides, if he loved you, he would have willingly taken you to the altar to bring GOD into the equation, but because he could not afford the whole you, he only wanted a piece of you, and that, my sister, should be an insult and a diss to you!

Deliverance
Deliverance is free. JESUS already paid the price. Ephesians 6:10-18 teaches us how to arm and protect

ourselves:

"Finally, my brethren, be strong in the Lord, and in the power of his might.

Put on the **whole armor** of God, that ye may be able to stand against the wiles of the devil.

For we wrestle not against flesh and blood, but against principalities, against powers, against the rulers of the darkness of this world, against spiritual wickedness in high places.

Wherefore take unto you the **<u>whole armor</u>** of God, that ye may be able to withstand in the evil day, and having done all, to stand.

Stand therefore, having your loins girt about with **truth**, and having on the breastplate of **righteousness**; And your feet shod with the preparation of the **gospel of peace**;

Above all, taking the **shield of faith**, wherewith ye shall be able to quench all the fiery darts of the wicked.

And take the **helmet of salvation**, and the **sword of the Spirit, which is the word of God**:

Praying always with all prayer and supplication **in the Spirit**, and **watching** thereunto with all **perseverance** and supplication for all saints."

Now, you'll notice that I have placed an emphasis on some words, because in our 'trained' reading styles, we tend to do just what we're taught. Read. That is, we say what we see, but we don't meditate on it.

There is no thought put into it. Let's break down the bold/underlined words.

Whole Armor of GOD:
One of the most common reasons for losing a battle against Satan is, saints tend to put on parts of the
armor, while leaving some parts exposed. Paul warned you in his letter to the Ephesians to put on the whole armor, and the armor is listed below and above this text.
First off, we HAVE to understand that we are not wrestling with the flesh! I have heard so many
women say they have a problem with their hormones and they couldn't live without sex. They have yet to understand that this is not a hormonal issu;, it is a whore-monal one. That is, it is a spirit called
perversion. You can hump yourself into rehab and still find this big bellied lust demon still asking
for satisfaction. Stop wrestling with your flesh and start coming up against it in the Spirit.
Besides, when you have an issue in the flesh, you should consider a fast. Pray on it.

Truth.
There is no way to fight the demon if you are not honest with yourself about having it. There is no way to fight or overcome this demon if it is connected to a lying spirit. (Truth is, you want to get delivered from both of them.) Stand today and tell the truth, not just about your spiritual condition, but in regards to everything. You must remember, the bible says when an unclean spirit goes out, it searches (paraphrasing) for another host, but finding none, it returns to its former one, bringing seven more spirits more evil than itself. Now, the bible did not say what kind of demons they would be. So, let's say, for example's sake,

you've gotten delivered from the demon of lust and you've even cast away that lying spirit, but because you didn't realize that the 'lying' demon posed a real problem, you begin to lie again. This is evidence that the demon is back at what it considers to be it's home: you. Not to mention, it has company! Mr. Lust is in the pit and bound there till Judgment Day, but Mr. Lie just brought you a brand new sparkling lust demon, and now, you're worse off than before. Now, you're wondering why you have this insatiable urge to 'try something different.'

Keep this: When the flesh is burning from within, it is evident that hell is alive and well. If it's not a holy desire between married couples, rebuke it.

Please note that a married woman can have a whore spirit and still be faithful to her husband! You have to remember, it's a spirit and not an act. She may have willed herself to do right, but deliverance is still needed! It may remain dormant for a while or for the rest of her life, but it is still there and it needs to be cast out.

Righteousness
This is not a bad word, saints. So many argue as to what righteousness is, many defining it to include themselves, while they bask in their sins. Righteousness is having the right behavior before the LORD. Righteousness is believing GOD, not just for some things, but for all. "For what saith the scripture? Abraham believed God, and it was counted unto him for righteousness." (Romans 4:3)

Put on love. Put on meekness. Diffuse offense. Slaughter jealousy. Just be and do what the LORD has called you to be and do, and if you fall, forgive. Forgive others and FORGIVE YOURSELF. Get back up again, repent and wash yourself off in the BLOOD and put back on the cloak of righteousness and do not take it off again.

Gospel of Peace.
Not the gossip. Not the complaining. Let your tongue speak blessings, and disassociate yourself from anyone that speaks any other language than that of peace! Definitely not one whose feet are quick to run to evil. If someone calls you, for example, to tell you that a fight is brewing on 7th street, hang up the phone and pray for the people in the fight. Why run that way unless you love the contentions of the enemy?
If they speak gossip, say, "No habla ignorance."
If they are complaining, say, "I'm not from the wilderness. I'm sorry. I don't speak that dialect."
If they speak any evil; speak love, speak the WORD. What happens? Just as those who were building the tower of Babel stopped building it when their language was confused, so will a gossiper, complainer or backbiter stop building foolishness on your doorsteps when you don't speak their language. Keep this truth in mind: Anything you allow anyone to erect in your ears is going to plant seeds in your heart.

Shield of Faith.
What you need to know:
"Now faith is the substance of things hoped for, the

evidence of things not seen." (Hebrews 11:1)
"So then faith cometh by hearing, and hearing by the word of God." (Romans 10:17)
Faith is not believing that it can come to pass, faith is believing that GOD will bring it to pass. One can believe a mountain can be moved, but one with faith will move the mountain. There is a difference in believing 'in' something and expectation.

If I told you I could send you something in the mail, you wouldn't look for it, because even though you believe that I can send it, you won't believe I will send it. However, if I told you I am going to send you something in the mail, chances are, you will believe me and go to check the mail often. Well, FATHER told you in HIS WORD what HE will do for you, but believing that 'HE can' do it won't move HIM. Believing that HE can and HE will do it for you, connects your faith to HIS WORD, and when the two become one, everything that is not of HIM has to divorce your reality. Faith comes by hearing and hearing by the WORD of GOD. Meaning, if you're not taking in the WORD, you have no WORD to pour out. Your challenge: Read your bible, go to bible study, go to Sunday service, pray often. Don't let another day go by where you tell yourself that you're going to do these things tomorrow. Make your today the day that you will begin to live in your newness.

Sword of the Spirit
This is, of course, the WORD of GOD. Now, let me clear something up. I hear a lot of people, when challenged say, "Devil, I rebuke you in the Name of

JESUS." JESUS is the LIVING WORD and
rebuke means to correct or express disapproval of. Now,
let's translate what they are saying. "Devil, I
don't like what you're doing (or saying) in the Name of
JESUS!" Now, don't you know that the enemy
is sitting up and laughing at your ignorance? What
correction did you just give him, except the ole
"Leave me alone" whimper? He doesn't have to because
you did not fashion the SWORD. You named
JESUS, but what did the WORD say about your situation
or challenge? Remember, when CHRIST
was taken atop a mountain to be tested by the devil. How
did CHRIST answer him? WITH THE
WORD! You want to wear the helmet of salvation, the
gospel of peace, girt your loins with truth, but
have no sword to fight with? So, now the devil is in hot
pursuit of you and you can't figure out how he can come
after you. You put on part of the armor, but you forgot to
pick up your weapon and that's why you're standing on the
battle field screaming, "Leave me alone!" In this fight,
you'd better bring your weapon!

Helmet of Salvation.
Quite frankly, you have to be saved. You have no right to
the FATHER if you haven't accepted the
SON.
How do I get saved?
BELIEVE, RECEIVE and CONFESS HIM
---"That if thou shalt confess with thy mouth the Lord
Jesus, and shalt believe in thine heart that God
hath raised him from the dead, thou shalt be saved."

(Romans 10:9)

DON'T GIVE UP OR GIVE IN NO MATTER WHAT!

---"But he that shall endure unto the end, the same shall be saved." (Matthew 24:13)

---"And ye shall be hated of all men for my name's sake: but he that shall endure unto the end, the same shall be saved." (Mark 13:13)

---"He that believeth and is baptized **shall** be **saved**; but he that believeth not **shall** be damned." (Mark 16:16)

Now that you know the armor, please pay attention to the methods.

Praying always is submitting to the MOST HIGH. The devil DOES NOT SLEEP! That's why GOD sternly warned us to pray without ceasing! Now, that isn't to pray for 24 hours, unless you're lead, but what this means is...You need to pray always...all times of the day and night...don't religiously set a schedule to pray. That's what the Pharisees and Scribes did. They prayed over their food, prayed before sleeping, prayed in the tabernacle, but there hearts were nowhere near GOD'S heart.

They were engaging in learned behavior. You need to pray at any and every moment that you are free to pray. You don't have to fall on your face at all times. You can pray in your car while driving, you can pray while you're browsing the Internet, you can pray in the shower or on the toilet. Don't schedule the LORD like HE'S your associate. HE'S FATHER! Talk to HIM. Even pray about what you're reading, what you're told...never trust information, trust HOLY GHOST confirmation!

Here are some additional steps that you should take:

1. If you have had sex with your 'boyfriend,' you have cursed the union because the sex was illegal.
Pray and ask the LORD that if it is not HIS will that this relationship continue, that HE end it
peacefully and give you both peace with the decision. GOD has to be that third fold in the cord and
because HE was not, a demonic strand has netted the two of you in a soul tie. Now, if the LORD
allows you to continue the relationship, (of course, the sex has to stop), that relationship is going to
have to go through 'deliverance' or consecration. I know you either think you love him or maybe you
do love him, but you HAVE to love GOD more and trust that HE has better plans for you than you do
for yourself.
2. Avoid any situations where you can have sex. That is, do not be alone together. I know how it is; in
the past, I lied to myself a lot too, saying, "Oh, if I just go over here, nothing is going to happen. We're going to
watch a little TV, eat some popcorn, and I'm going home." If you put yourself in a place where your flesh can
overwhelm you, it will. Just because you hung out with a man for seven days and didn't do anything, does not mean
you can continue. Believe me, if he loves you, he will not find this offensive, because in his mind, you are his wife to
be. So, why waste time trying to fit someone into a place that GOD has carved for someone else? Don't you know
that the only way a puzzle piece can fit into a place that it is not designed to be, is if it is obstructed? No more alone
time; but just phone time and hanging out in public.
3. Kisses? No way. Now, in today's world, kissing is

widely accepted, but why are you trading saliva
with a man who can possibly be someday the husband of
another woman? Kissing does lead to sex.
4. If your 'friend' is insistent about having sex with you
because he says, "You're going to marry each
other anyway," or "No one wants to buy a vehicle that they
haven't driven," (I'm not going to sugar coat this) break up
with him and disassociate yourself. This is evidence that
he is not your husband or this is not your season to be with
him. You see, GOD only picks the fruit and put them in a
basket together when they are ripe and obviously, he's not
ready yet.
5. Repent of all of your sins, both known and unknown.
That is, allow the LORD to turn your heart
from the sin and apologize for it. How do you turn from it?
By getting WORD in relation to that sin in you until your
mind is changed. Then you can 'truly' be sorry.
6. Ask the FATHER to cover you with the BLOOD of
JESUS. An Israelite (Levite--Priest) had to be
consecrated before he went before the LORD. He couldn't
just walk up in HIS presence. JESUS is the
WAY, the TRUTH and the LIGHT and no man cometh to
the FATHER except by HIM!
7. Ask the LORD to fill you with HIS HOLY SPIRIT and
begin to worship HIM.
8. Now bring your issue before HIM.
Please note that all demons don't go out straight-way or
immediately. JESUS told HIS Disciples in
Matthew 17:21, in relation to the boy with the epileptic
demon, "Howbeit this kind goeth not out but by prayer and
fasting." Therefore, you may have to fast as well. Ask the

LORD or fast until HE takes you off of it. Don't worry. HE will be with you. Don't give up. Don't give in.

How does one press charges against this spirit? Now, of course, we have already listed the steps to deliverance, however, the bible tells us, *"When the unclean spirit is gone out of a man, he walketh through dry places, seeking rest, and findeth none. Then he saith, I will return into my house from whence I came out; and when he is come, he findeth it empty, swept, and garnished. Then goeth he, and taketh with himself seven other spirits more wicked than himself, and they enter in and dwell there: and the last state of that man is worse than the first. Even so shall it be also unto this wicked generation."* (Matthew 12:43-45)

An unclean spirit, or demon doesn't just see you as a person, a soul, or a child of GOD; it sees you as a piece of property with an appointment with destruction. It wants to keep you so that you do not miss this appointment. There is no love between it and you. It hates you because it hates your FATHER, so to retaliate against HIM, it seeks to destroy the very ones in which HE loves. According to the scriptures, once it has been cast out, it seeks refuge somewhere else and when it does not find any, it comes back in search of you. It finds you delivered, a new creature in CHRIST and it goes out and brings back seven more spirits more evil than itself. It wants to make sure that you do not get away again! It wants to ensure that you meet your date with death and eventually stand in the pit of hell along with it. So, of course, you want to ensure that it does not come back. How do you do this?

PRESS CHARGES!

Now, of course, you cannot pick up the phone and dial 911 and report a spiritual attack, unless you want to be escorted from your home in a straight jacket. GOD is FATHER, the ALPHA and OMEGA, the CREATOR of all living things, therefore, everything in and on this earth is in subjection to HIM. HE is the GREAT LAWMAKER. Take your issue before HIM and remain innocent in it! That demon has committed multiple crimes against HIM and you. First off, allowing itself to follow Satan, but in your case, it put its hands on you, when GOD strictly warned, *"Touch not mine anointed, and do my prophets no harm."* (Psalms 105:15) He has broken the law! But, you, being more than a conqueror (never think yourself to be a victim), have to know the WORD in order to bring charges up against that spirit. And, one of his crimes was touching you. Secondly, to keep the crime from being committed against you again, or against your children or their children, you have to bind (imprison) the spirit. We'll just call it Citizens Arrest! In the earth realm, you are the citizen, the judge and the warden! *"Know ye not that we shall judge angels? How much more things that pertain to this life?"* (1 Corinthians 6:3) Therefore, you have the right to arrest that spirit by binding it. Don't let it bind you anymore! Now, there is sentencing. Of course, GOD has already sentenced it to hell for eternity, however, GOD allows you to exact a right-now sentence against it. *"Verily I say unto you, Whatsoever ye shall bind on earth shall be bound in heaven: and whatsoever ye shall loose on earth shall be loosed in heaven."* (Matthews 18:18) BIND IT AND CAST IT INTO THE PIT (ABYSS) AND BIND IT THERE UNTIL THE DAY OF JUDGMENT, IN JESUS NAME! You see, you have the power and the GOD given authority to do this! Be sure to bind any replacements from being sent up against you or your family or sent out.

Now, live in your freedom, binding up any demon that comes your way. Children start exhibiting the characteristics of the spirit of whoredom? Bind the spirit! Spouse starts getting a little 'weird' and perverted? Bind the spirit! Manager starts getting goo goo eyed at you? Bind the spirit! GOD has given you the right to act as Sheriff, and your body, spirit and soul is your country to protect. Don't let any demon come into it and spray graffiti on your heart and put blindfolds on your eyes. It's time for you to go and act as the head and not the tail, because you are!

ARREST WARRANT

SUPERIOR COURT OF THE KINGDOM OF HEAVEN
ARREST AFFADAVIT
Your Name Here
vs.

The Spirit of Whoredom
Case Number: 7 (Completion)
Prosecutor Listed: The WORD of GOD
Plaintiff: Your Name Here
Defendant: Spirit of Whoredom
Judge:
EL SHADDAI (GOD ALMIGHTY)
ELOHIM
EL-ELYON (MOST HIGH GOD)
EL-ROI (STRONG ONE WHO SEES)
JEHOVAH-SHALOM (THE LORD IS PEACE)
JEHOVAH--YAHWEH (THE LORD SAVES)
Charges in Indictment:
Touching GOD's anointed
Harming GOD's Prophets
Illegal Alien
Theft
(More charges are pending against the above named
defendant from this Plaintiff and others)
Plaintiff also requests a restraining order.
In addition, defendant has requested a restraining order
against the defendant. He claims that the
defendant, beat him by praising the LORD, mocked him by
saying what GOD said and not what he
caused, called in a gang of prayer warriors, praisers and

worshipers, who in term beat the defendant even more and bound him. Defendant claims that he tried to flee the scene, but was pursued by Angels and thrown into court, however, because of the Plaintiff's prayers, he is unable to continue harassing,
killing, tormenting and burglarizing other souls that he had access to. Defendant also requests a change
of venue, stating that with GOD, he could not possibly get a fair trial.
Plaintiff's Request: Approved
Defendant's Request: Denied

Made in the USA
Columbia, SC
11 November 2024

46182749R10057